SPIRIT MATTERS

SPIRIT MATTERS

White Clay, Red Exits, Distant Others

poems by

GORDON HENRY

Holy Cow! Press
Duluth, Minnesota
2022

Author photograph by Kimberly Blaeser.
Cover painting, "The Storyteller, Spiritual Sex," by Jim Denomie.
Cover and book design by Anton Khodakovsky.

Printed and bound in the United States of America.
ISBN 978-1737405122

First printing, Spring, 2022

Library of Congress Cataloging-in-Publication Data
Henry, Gordon, 1955- author.
Spirit matters : white clay, red exits, distant others / poems by Gordon Henry.
Duluth, Minnesota : Holy Cow! Press, 2022.
LCCN 2021049122 | ISBN 9781737405122 (trade paperback)
LCGFT: Poetry.
LCC PS3558.E4974 S65 2022 | DDC 811/.54--dc23/eng/20211105
LC record available at https://lccn.loc.gov/2021049122

10 9 8 7 6 5 4 3 2 1

Holy Cow! Press projects are funded in part by grant awards from the Ben and Jeanne Overman Charitable Trust, the Elmer L. and Eleanor J. Andersen Foundation, the Lenfestey Family Foundation, the Woessner Freeman Family Foundation, and by gifts from generous individual donors. We are grateful to Springboard for the Arts for their support as our fiscal sponsor.

Holy Cow! Press books are distributed to the trade by Consortium Book Sales & Distribution, c/o Ingram Publisher Services, Inc., 210 American Drive, Jackson, TN 38301.
For inquiries, please write to: Holy Cow! Press, Post Office Box 3170, Mount Royal Station, Duluth, MN 55803.
Visit *www.holycowpress.org*

For the Good Day people, the good life givers, my relatives, my beautiful partner Mary Anne, my daughters Kehli, Mira and Emily, my granddaughters Elliana, Kora and Kyla, my teachers and helpers, Francis Cree, Louis Cree, Rose Cree and those still living Adisokan we carry in words and stories from the beginning we all came from and continue toward.

Miigwetch to the late Basil Johnston, for his work *The Manitous: The Spiritual Worlds of the Ojibways*, wherein he reminded us of the older spirits of stories, especially the Adisokan of stillness and music, Cheeby-aub-oozoo.

All poems and artwork in this publication are in compliance with the Indian Arts and Crafts Act. Beware "Faux Skins," as written about in a poem by Heid Erdrich.

In memory of Jim Denomie (1955-2022), with gratitude for his art and vision, in thanks for ways his work has imaginatively inspired and creatively sustained so many of us for so many years, living with us and through us in the spirit of creation.

TABLE OF CONTENTS

AS IF WHITE CLAY 1

Prologue 3

Untitled 4

Relative X: 6
A White Clay
Tabernacle of Grief

Abstract on Reminders 8

Sighted In—Another Eye of 12
Memory, Fall Again

With a Rifle, a Flask 15

The Return of 17
White Clay Brothers

From the Book of Zahquod, 18
Letter Niizh

Dear Venus Zhaawanigiizhik 20

Dear Uncle X 21

Venus Zhaawanigiizhik 23
(One of the Triplet Aunts)

Through the Refuge 25

Departure: 29
A White Clay Soldier

Venus Zhaawanigiizhik: 31
How I Learned To Love

Crow Woman You Dreamt 33
Dark from the Name of Fire

It Was Snowing 34
on the Monuments

Spirit Matters 35

This is How Your Great 37
Uncle Dies

Zahquod Reaches Through 39
the Hospital Wall to Fire

INTERLUDE: 41
Waterlogue, Spirit,
Containers, Bodies

Living Water Lullaby 43
for Dead Settler Language

Waterlogue Prelude: 45
The Art of Water

Dead Settler Waterlogue 46

The River Tells, 50
Sings to Us Sleeping

COUNTLESS RED EXITS 55

A Dark Bar 56
Near a Poison River

Dead GPS 58

August Again 59

Book of Samuel, Chapter   61
Zahquod—Page Unknown

Another Spirit Fire   63
Under Empire

Back Before We Returned   65
to White Clay

The Archer Uncle   67

This Will Be Your Last   69
Ceremony, You Think

Spirit Matters: In   70
Remembrance

Shadow Boxes for Zahquod   72

Suddenly Cousin X   75

Uncle X   76

Venus Zhaawanigiizhik   78
Tries to Kill (POV Uncle X)

INTERLUDE: 83
An Uncertain Longing

Broken Table of Contents   85
From Zahquod's
Book of Dreams

The Song I Wanted   86
to Write is Traveling

DISTANT OTHERS   87

Letter to Cousin X   89

Among the Almost   90
Decolonized

The Mute Scribe Recalls   92
Some Talking Circle

We Regurgitate   94
Diagnoses

I Have Streamed the Arcane   96
Mother Tongue

The Ailing Medicine   98
Comedian's Postcolonial
Death Song

Large Provocative Answers   102

Given the Crows   104
Gliding Above Me

Mahtoha's Futile Attempt   107
to Decolonize the Western
History Meeting

Speak Dear Desert Crow   109

Postcolonial Dream Abstract   110
(Blue Shadow Uncle Sings
the Sun Down)

Venus Zhaawanigiizhik   112
Once Said

Love Letter 113
Delivered by Muskrat

I Want to See You 115

Catalonian Square, 116
Palms and Light

The Lake Up North 118

What Remains 119

Dear Firefly 120

Memory Song 122
for a Woman at the
Southern Door

Rain I Almost Remember 124

Only Lyric Remains 125
Capable

Sovereignly Erotica 126

Uncle X Like Virgil Needs 128
His Own Guide

Passing Thoughts Over a 131
Fire (Dear Crow Woman)

(Dear Crow Woman) 137

Clues to My 139
Own Silence

Book of Samuel—Chapter 140
Zahquod, Page Unknown

Zahquod—My Last Letter 141

Crushed Akiiwenzii 144
(A Disintegrating
Grandfather Hologram)

Letter to Zahquod, 146
Spirit Matters

Let Us Be Painting, Painter, 150
Singing, Singing, Singer
For H.E. Ephemera

Try Not to Say Essence 151

Venus Zhaawanigiizhik: 152
Soliloquy

At Times the Distant Other 153

Yet to Be Unnamed Arrival 154

Epilogue: 156
Chiaaboos at
the River Again

Acknowledgments 159

About the Author 161

AS IF
WHITE
CLAY

PROLOGUE

(Chiaaboos at the River)

Yes water's edge may give you a song
And cedar another breath of prayer
But don't forget the shadows as sun
Goes down in flicker fall of sparrows
A last view before the sun leaves for
The to of morrow
The closing eye
Of the storyteller
Breathing syllables of
Another beginning to tell of
In the wash and rock of the
Possible all in the improbable
Awe of him or her, they, the who
Of whatever the story comes through
at widening shore of dream
Drawing forth a vessel unshaped
Shipping light drifting to take us
Back from where we came
The way of dream
The way of dreamers
Dreaming without
Knowing a way

UNTITLED

The story you wanted to write is on fire
paper lathered with bear grease
floating down a river

Your
Aunt on the other side
of the river a phone to her ear
chewing gum howling obscenities
into a mouthpiece under thunder
heads emerging in shapes that will
inspire names of children yet to know language

The other end earpiece?

Your
Grandfather
underground in a funereal shadow box
surrounded by liquor glass a few jagged
bottle bottoms, throats broken from empties,
the rest crushed stars of ice, brown grain
belt toenails, curved claws of windshield
glass blown open from some long night
of lost impact, an abused blue Buick
carrying a body heading for the star
road afterlies, afterlife

the container and (un)contained
reshaped like memory itself pieced
chaotically in chips and mounds of images
too treacherous to touch, too sharp to

hold, too broken to make out the seen
their shining, less so, if they even show
anything, but how the moon or sun still
move across the time wrought surfaces
we are and have been on the way
to submergence a deeper drawing down
of face into glass
glass and eyes
eyes lost
in fixed gaze
of some turned over interior
seeing may never come back from

Relative X:
A White Clay
Tabernacle of Grief

of longing, unwrapped parcels of lost joy,
survival school books, margins
with poorly drawn broken hearts, empty
mirrors, wash basin and rear view, useless
timepieces, worn down to a last hour an
interval less than a stopped second

Tobacco ties, bowls of beads for unmade
giveaway thunderbirds, BIA checkstubs
A glass ashtray your mother threw at some
deer hunter shadow of betrayal in the
doorway

A hissing cassette recording of *Ring of Fire*
sung by the army vet face on the drunk
punch wall, who waved the gun at
us last Christmas then set fire to his own
childhood regalia

There's an unblessed host in there too,
a book of matches from some white bar in
Walker, Park Rapids or Wadena, a poorly
developed photo of a blonde from Anoka,
a page lifted from the *Invisible Musician*,
a baseball cup, a Kennedy half dollar from
a confirmation sponsor, an illegible prescription
for persistent pain, the dried white
chrysanthemum, wedding flower, a bullet

from the pistol your aunt threw into
the white clay river, after your grandfather died,
a singer's drumstick from the drum, with
only one living singer left

ABSTRACT ON REMINDERS

All around
US
(drinking personae)
Virgil who crossed over
the river running
carrying everybody
into star formations
Zahquod who followed
Joe V. . . .
A few years later
their ball gloves
and dog tags where
we left them long ago
under the wooden
backboard

Dawn
licking salt and tears
from windows east
and west
In black cast iron stove
rooms stoked to
the warmth of old people
Last night's
cards on the table
left fanned out
a pair of diamonds
no less

Light breaking into
squawk and squalls of

8

flight and fall of the smallest
of nameless birds

Lest naming
become an exercise

Become
reminders
all around
US
(talking personae)
This happened then
this the letters never
arrived after we lost
our language
we couldn't afford the
phone we couldn't hear
ourselves through
any way one voice
to another remains
the distance between
war and home

Reminders all
around US
(The eating
personae) of some
table of some time
ago the child
the cereal
consuming the words
on the box face

patting the bread
with grease
folgers in the throat
the uncle saying
the gun

Reminders
all around
US
(the killing personae)
in the closet
your grandfathers
deer rifle
heart attack regalia
beadwork and fringed
buckskin jacket
hanging there with
no one to wear it
or with no wish to put
it on.

This is how we all
must depart
Reminders
all around
US
(Left for dead
personae)
clothes a hat
maybe
keys to an older vehicle
photos pleading

when we happen to look
please burn
A woodstove waiting
to be lit again

SIGHTED IN—ANOTHER EYE OF MEMORY, FALL AGAIN

Your Uncle Soldier
X stands
on concrete steps
just outside the front door
sighting in his rifle

After a morning of ricing
an afternoon draining Grain Belts
and sundown filled with silver
shots of gin and more a few
sky glazed tumblers
of seagrams

He tells you

The bullet pocked stop sign
signs how he aims at loss
the Fond du Lac woman
he loved most
who took his keys
wrecked his galaxy
spinning out of control
on ice cracking road

He sees enemies' heads set
on tree branches
bodies of war, his and others
slithering through brush

emerging with bar fight ghosts

He Imagines you imagine
faces smirking insults and slights
rising up out of reeds
beyond the roadside creek
and aims there too

Wired mourning doves
coo above
the low weeping voice
of his punched out
bruised mother

A crow fleeing roadkill on
the pavement beneath
at the report of his rifle

Within his vision each bark
eye of tree peers out as
another memory sighted in

So, with this evening
he sights and shoots

A tethered dog howls
beyond the four-corner stop
near the survival school

A bullet travels half moonlight
clear stars spinning off behind
whirring, whizzing

over a darkening field

Toward some distant stone
where he once sat
alone waiting for his
Father to come out
of the woods, dragging
a young buck

Eyes gone glassy opaque
gazing to dimming
reflections of trees
an unknown beyond

That nearly forgotten
bullet of memory
firing misplaced desire
another round of recall
boring toward the old man
now

With a last drunken shot

A flutter above
The boy still on the stone

Less than a murder of crows
rising, dispersing west
autumn violet in
the night side of
dusk

WITH A RIFLE, A FLASK

While carrying the shadow of
a wounded father on his back
your uncle
jabs and feints with
your air hooking
Aunt

Who later pulls rosaries
from the wall
and passes them among
Us.

Hearts and Spades
card games
after that

Until doorways filled
with shadows
return to us

With a rifle, a flask
of what might
have better been

Forgotten like
hunger impatient
for more of the same
food

We've all grown
skins thick as the thin

barriers between
the rooms
our bodies have
made fit for hiding.

THE RETURN OF WHITE CLAY BROTHERS

      Two-nights gone skins
Dark as discarded
sunned Grain
Belt bottles
      Both mouthing names
      Sheets lost to the wind
Wandering up a two track
in a village of smoking stoves
burnt remains of machinery
Grass and weeds where
drivers now dead once steered
toward lights where the old
woman still living still settles

Children beneath star
blankets the eyes of each
rapt as if the Story about
to be told were standing
beyond the fixed doorway
darkening
outside waiting to enter.

FROM THE BOOK OF ZAHQUOD, LETTER NIIZH

It was the Dakota
border winter Bear
slept with Smoke and Mirrors
Woman

You had made fire from
receipts, the cloth of ancestors
and wrappings of gifts
crumpled into condensed
versions of stories of
children's forgotten wishes

Of nothing more
to say between us
Your songs were holding
you in spaces of cultural
relevance and mine in
prolonged absorption
of a ceremonial rigor
of driving between
your treatment and
frozen roads home

Work had buried
dogs and in-laws
in the shadows of
trees making masks
from sundown running

distant engines
into the hills

Let's forget our diseases
the strings winding us
in decay and desperate
attempts to remember

I still have this beating
animal to face each morning
asking me for bread and wine
a story to tell against the
loss and lies
As if love would ever
come around again
As if that was where all
this began.

Dear Venus Zhaawanigiizhik

Your last letter broke up in shadows
for words I could not read
like all who wake and sleep
I am a poor translation between light
and dark

Quote Dear lost ellipses of the lost End quote

Ellipses of your dead nephew
The rez housing son/daughter ellipses
Winter whimpers for IHS prescriptions ellipse
What your grandfather said
on Stone Child Road endquote

How you wrote of cold turns to
another death sentence another
still younger Son ellipses deep
burning liver scars ellipses at 40

Quote sincerely Endquote
I see now what the shadows do
What remains too much for light to
translate may be all I can see

I suppose you will return in winter
seeking another relative for another
place to reside, another body to lay with
as your sweetness I remember made
me want to forget this life for a love
ellipses without hope.

DEAR UNCLE X

These lines are too much like the world we spoke of, like stoned out bragging in basements, in the rhetorical fissures of decorated walls, the whether or nots just blowing about, talking war, world, third, first second, the prospects of discovery, the projections of the cold inner theatre, that one that talks to you before the red velvet curtain, that one that speaks before the windows prop, blinds, slatternly shadow, sun, shadow, sun, beside the wall of photographs, momentary masks you wore to wear time down to a final aperture, the sleeping field, winter, tracks of animals, over flowers and snow covered stone, little faded flags blowing about on sticks.

Shall I tell you my story, the one of grief, the one of deception, the one of travel, the one of the talk over a wooden table after a funeral, the one of the glass draining rum into a face just beyond reach in the dark? Should I tell you the story of the one I wanted to shoot, the one I wanted to love, the white feather falling from the sky, the search on the other side of the river for the lost child, the Uncle who wanted to kill your mother, the North Dakota prayers ties, on the tree we gave tea to, before we cut it. Shall I tell you the one about the ugly fights over missing articles, ownership of clothes and cars and the heart attack regalia your father wore, at the grand entry where he died? Shall I tell of the one, following the old man to a yellow house in winter where he ate with other women and woke up one Sunday to find you sleeping in a snowed over driveway, as he made his way to mass. Shall I tell you the one about the altar boy latin I could not memorize, not the words you've seen like e pluribus unum, or semper fi, or vedi, vici veni, but a whole fucking confeitor, the complete god damned lords prayer, all the litanies, the hymns, the gospels, the Friday rules. Shall I tell that one?

Every one is great here. We've burned all the firewood you cut last year. Your sister gave me your rifle. I've looked down the scope a few times and saw people walking down the road, a dog pissing on a tree, a yellow sign with holes in it, already shot at, a shirt on a line, like the one you used to wear when you went out with that Leech Lake woman, a boy across the road shooting hoops, the red galaxy you got from the old man, turned over in the yard, a cross still hanging from the rear view mirror inside, I looked hard down the scope, there was nothing worth shooting at.

Days are still numbers here, this one if I remember correctly, is a long one, day not number, just after Christmas, the 27th, no the 28th. I have to go now, the door just blew open, I hear a phone, the coffee's done, there are no words left for this day, I'm leaving like I always do, when silence and time get too deep, I go back among these people you too wanted so badly to love.

Venus Zhaawanigiizhik (One of the Triplet Aunts)

Calls

the last person
in White Clay
to have spoken through
a ghost telephone
on a wall

Not then as we would
Now

to someone on the road west
a clear voice singing
a turtle mountain healing song
marked and transmitted by
towers and satellites

But then as not
Now

to the distant father
breathing heavy and fast
over hard liquor under low light
from some west coast
bay area bar

Wound whether through wire
through time less

timelessness we remain
connected even when we
have gone so far west as to make
everything even the better
and worst of memory
out of something signaling us
to the almost out of reach

THROUGH THE REFUGE

The roads here hold
more than memory
can take us to

Horizons packed with
cloud backed pines
Turns opening to

Waterways
signs of an ancient flood
of tears
overseen by nesting
eagles now

Another horizon then
gray clouds rippling
over Green Lake
over thin stands of
Round Lake rice
combed by thin
brushes of
western breeze

Then a left turn
toward the funeral
past dance grounds
the tribal school
the cemetery
the catholic church

Gathering relatives
some still fighting
over possessions
The dead leave

Boxes, letters,
photographs by
the decades
Absent bodies
a mix of faces,
the living and
the already
passed

An address book buried
beneath
legal instructions on
belongings for
an executor

Deeper, grievers, some
half-sisters
Long-faced longing
for a few artifacts

The winnowing basket
one of a set
from otter tail pillager
Grandparents

A fistful of jewels from
a St. Cloud suitor from
outside the family
One of the men
the dead woman
married once

During the service
In the survival school
Gymnasium
Someone says
We should not speak
Her name now
She's Traveling
Traveling
She is Traveling
on that big star
road

Someone older
at my side
in the bleachers
another ex
a dakota with
an eagle staff

Whispers
"she spoke
used to speak, fluently
at night
in the language
while dreaming

I didn't understand
but she was smiling
in her sleep
I thought maybe
she was dreaming
of something like
love, something like
that."

DEPARTURE:
A WHITE CLAY SOLDIER

All whispers begin and end
at departures of secrets
and trust

At the fenceless Cemetery
with a stone pillar
entryway

We stand here now
as old men of war fire
off guns they store
In closets and carry
through
the best stories
dreams create
of bravery and hunts

The air then holds
all
every report
returning from flash
and smoke

To quiet
relatives
leaving for a feast
enough to sustain
them as they too
must travel home.

As for you Uncle X
Stone will carry
your name and let
it lie just this side
of that old spirit house
under the long standing
pine

VENUS ZHAAWANIGIIZHIK: HOW I LEARNED TO LOVE

Morning sings from another
black iron stove mouth
of some oak arms blazing
in a fireplace
made to withstand
Incinerating speeches of rez edge
fundamentalist preachers
who want you to divest
from the skin you left
hanging with all of us who
have been taken to urban
and urbane life the dirtier
cleaners by uber, para taxis
yellow, checker, nixon, dog,
reagan, 401k9 militias, commanded
by the cold tweets of the cryogenic
plutocrats who count
lies in equations insoluble
(poor) equals deserved dead
(rich) equals (entitlement) minus
(everyone else is) null (as void)

Let me speak of last night
raining glass and fists, wolf's tail
shitstorm spiral in the white eye
of the someone spouting
john 3:16 or some other jesus
christ biblio-code for settler
salvation

Even as Morning sings with Morning
Glory trumpets as age eats
broken bones of the one eared
woman who takes my money
deep into the future even as
we made love in the past, the present
still splitting infinitives, a horizon
that cannot hold the light through
a window broken by flat screen
television i've learned to call by
the name of real love

A White Clay woman named Venus
Zhaawanigiizhik who I left
at the Greyhound
Station, her face deep into
a paper bag
of medicine
we've all been
warned about

CROW WOMAN YOU DREAMT DARK FROM THE NAME OF FIRE

held horizon to memory of long flights over enemy hills

I talk long distance to a relative dying for something better already gone with the thought of something worse

Than this last pine quiet room that final turn of conversation in the burning hills beyond glassed in ghosts

the language lost between us with no more light to hold our seeing anything but the door we might already have closed

Without a word ready to follow without a word to lead us a body without earth a home without land just wind walking dogs and shaking leaves a shock of thunder to come.

It Was Snowing on the Monuments

My dead father's name next to my living mothers

You went further back into the cemetery
There where so many lies remain lost to winter

There with the named and the nameless
It was snowing on the monuments

All horizons packed with cloud cover
bodies
Some of us left in the vehicles
we came in

Some became some final gesture
of departure's sun borne reflect
behind auto glass
heat blowing feeling back into a face

It was snowing on the monuments
Even in the warmth of an engine turning over
You must forget how we came to this place
how we leave

SPIRIT MATTERS

In relatives red exits
From government day schools
Entrances to Tribal operations
IHS waiting areas
Theaters in White border towns
Basketball floors set up for wakes
Traveling songs
urging relatives toward
the lasting grace of
Star Road narratives

From matter of turned over vehicles
boxes run empty
over asphalt far from home
Spirit crow echo dark hinged
to memory too deep for even love to tell

Matter the fuselage for the
Sparked projections of all
unsettled trash left
roadside and before that
Made even the sublime of product
into packages left over as
the consumed gone
the unconsumed a breath of
matter too dense
to die by fire or flood, quake or violence
of winds forced enough to lift anybody from any
place on earth's enduring ever giving
ever revealing face

Turning again and again
In spirit giving
turning again and ever again
revealed by an
ever giving spirit of
shine and long
and evermore light
all matter carries in arrivals and
exits
Carries away
In seeming singular
making and unmaking

THIS IS HOW YOUR GREAT UNCLE DIES

You meet tradition again
in an airport waiting area
this time an old Cree

A Stone Child sculptor
a Masters in Visual Arts
a self-determination birthdate
syllabary sequence tattoo
peeking out
From a rolled up
Pearl button sleeve cuff

Returning to Billings
A Sports bar layover in Minneapolis
A slow beginning conversation
with ice falling into
a glass with two
fingers of hard, burning
silences until

The old man
lights a fire

"Where you from?"

Turns to tribes bleeding
into people and gatherings
in common

Ends with
21st Century memories

Ceremonies
old and gone thirst
dance witnesses

no longer fasting in
arbors he will no
longer go into

He's going back to that
place he should have never left
me leaving for a place
I should never return to.

It wasn't some Indigenous
knowledge that killed the old
man or some grief gap
We fell into
it was what leads
to the slickly missed
turn of road
into an ice cracking
river
at the end of the
headlights of a gold
Impala

ZAHQUOD REACHES THROUGH
THE HOSPITAL WALL TO FIRE

Casting crows among dispersions, dispersions the voices of three men
tending fire, Singer, Johnny Liar and Uncle X, all dead.

The drugs fully charged medications for different histories of cells held
captive by shadow traumas, the beatings, the leavings by car and death.
Cells that will eat you inside out someday

For you a kidney dissolves before you can enter another
century of lost talk

You hang out by fire for a while just to exit from
the Singers spell not quite riding away in song
part of you wants to remain to stay with
Fire

Part of you never liked where everything was headed
in what others were saying about you in illness
in the very spaces where you held their faces

More than once saying over and over again
I need you to let me rest, just rest, rest
with this, just rest for a while
The fire is good, warm, sit, look to it
while I rest and keep resting until I know
nothing more than what it is to rest

INTERLUDE:

Waterlogue, Spirit,
Containers, Bodies

LIVING WATER LULLABY
FOR DEAD SETTLER LANGUAGE

By the ancient sea
Of name said water

Stood an ancient you
With no sun above

Could the past be
Said to be well
Behind

You the name
In the sea said
Water

Look to the road
To the hill
Up that way

Follow the call
Forget what may
Be

The voice of
Some ancient
The sea said water

Without love
Without without
The speaking

Inside won't
Speak about

The you the
Name the past
That be

Inside an ancient
Thee the sea
Said water

All the lost
of language
Tongues
Touched surface

A thirst
Wails though
You've made
The mountain

More of echo
Than source
Than named

From high above
Words soft
Wind blow

Back down
Back down
To sea said
Water.

WATERLOGUE PRELUDE:
THE ART OF WATER

becomes Shapeless
water
becomes colorless
Imageless
water
becomes soundless
water becomes
tasteless water
becomes
particles, bodies
holds the living
held by the living
to live through water
to live to flow
as light as water
just as older once
living parts live now
parts of this living
continuous stream illumined
at times by moon yet
not seen in brightness
of sun

DEAD SETTLER WATERLOGUE

Holy Water
Baptismal Fount Water
Typewriter font Water
Found Water
Divination Water
Mountain Water
Waste Water
Water you be waiting for
Narcissus Water
Wife of Bath Water
Flies Water
Calyx Water
Bird Bath Water
Po et ree waw ter
Skinny Dipping Water
Mama Dipping Achilles Water
Iceberg Water

Sink Water
Backwater
Lunar Path Water
Urine Water
I'm in Water
Dog Bowl Water
Fire Water
Bubbling Brook Water
Water Like the sound of Thunder
Thunder Water
Bottled Water
Canned Water
Water soluble
Making Water

Talking water
Swamp Water
Big crock of Water
Holding your water

Water carrier
Water Walkers
Rainwater
Brain Water
Swamp Water
Water Dipper
Cistern water
Watered down
Water town
Waterbury
Upstream Water
Water of life
Cup of Water
Water tower
Water skimmers
Water colors
Water Views
Water's edge
Water Current
Water falls
Breaking pregnancy
Water
Water mark
Watervliet
Laughing Water
Land of sky blue water
Water

Edge water
Ground water
Water boarding
Running water
Rushing water
Sunny Beach water
Well water
Water pump
Water Sports
Water guns
Water balloons
Water slides
Watermark
Water-bed
Ice water
Spring Water
Oil and water
Polluted Water
Water dripping from hotel eaves

Tap water
Dishwater
Waterwheel
Water park
Water pistol
Water hose
Water Skis
Underwater
Loon water
Smoke on the water
Black water
Oil slick water

Water crisis
Table water
Sparkling water
Tonic water
Potable water
Water Jug
Water soluble

River water
Water lily
Watercress
Litorally
Lake water
Sea to Shiny Sea
Ocean water
Blood in the water
To Wine
To Blood
Immersion in water
No life without
water
wet
wetter
unda
aqua
apah
julep
us as living
watercourse
of a language
losing its way
to our speechless
source

The River
Tells, Sings to Us
Sleeping

Fox on the right bank
before willow

Low flying crow across
ever flowing glisten
of our many faces

Leaping autumn spawn

The language of
strangers upstream

Something about
a moon cast echo
of a singer on a bridge

A canto of
blown smoke

With a syntax of floating bodies
and undisclosed submersible
consonance

This is where you may swim
This where you must not

A silent swirl here

A man and woman
on a red blanket
embankment together

A woman looking
into
stiller water
for a past
among floating
leaves

I have taken children
I have delivered relatives

Downstream from
portages and dams

A mother with
an offering to
always

Deer lick sunrise

We have accepted another
small craft

Washed out bear
tracks with the
wake of a white
canoe

Early moon at the bow
late Sun stern

Tales of missing
bodies and boats
Turned over
log rolling
narratives

Ice jam explosions

Torches and spears

The lunge of brown fish
Their sun streamed variant
color
the pull of line

A stones-throw splash

Underwater gleam of
small change

The entry of face wash
hands

 A skimmers touch
beneath a dragonfly
circle

The sand full lens
of a Canon caressed

by fingers of weed

The hardness of
protruding Rock
at heart stopping
rapids

A tuber's
beer can flying
toward the two
blue heron
priested shore

A hand on a lantern
drawing nearer to
this voice

A child looking to cross
an archipelago of
stones

A wine soaked
teenage poet
from the left bank
cursing loneliness

A leather notebook
turning over in cedar
leaf rapids
words illegible
a few unbound
pages separating

A zodiac pitcher
pouring star tailed
myths into all we
witness in slow
continuous passing

COUNTLESS
RED EXITS

A Dark Bar
Near a Poison River

From hole
in winter cloud
Eagle drops in midflight
Possum forgets fish smell
in garbage
Racoon
leaves her mask
dancing
away from a pile of
shit and steel
moose runs loose along
highway 61 through
ruins of an old drive-in
the screen wedged open
by moonlight
Crow swallows another
Timepiece as

People remember the
names
of clans in cartoon
episodes of good against
up against the wall
of not so good

as the failure of
everything we ordered
by mail or phone or text
or by Imperial jesus, or from

some other transactional
god to save us from failure

Those of us who still
have what the colonizers
called heart (they
longed to eat)
are still trying to sing
our organs back to life
back to our bodies
floating along
knowing this river
we are on
carries the wrong name
on all the maps
and in legends we
continue to inhabit

DEAD GPS

Cold white moon hanging
trees and shadows

You were talking about your
Sister, mother, or brother

Unheard of since you returned
from the iron door asylum

A school for excavation of dreams,
like those singers voices beyond touch
at play in a theatre of unwritten
codes, every gesture, agony
lost among lost fear lost

replaced with a continuing
Sense of moving between boxes
Vehicles we rename for lost
Relatives surrounded
by names of strangers
and numbers neither ordinal
or serial

Then auto light
sprays out
Coyote on dirt road

then just us again
wondering
where we are

AUGUST AGAIN

In the village of dead pines
and burnt up machinery

Power steals
a name with
every broken empty
bottle

past the abandoned
drive-in theatre

The road North draws
traffic to Shooting Star

signs of forgotten
country

music legends pulsing
larger in pixels
than life

Dark liquored skins,
substitute laughter

For hope another vice
for entertainment

Back home
I sleep next to fire and feed
the old Man
sleeping with the rifle

his heart attack regalia
hanging in a closet

wrapped in plastic
warming with the blanket
a now dead nephew stood on
for a summer naming

Perhaps we have killed you. Filled you with words, stuffed your body and sent you off, in a bottle, on a raft, tied to an arrow, boxed perhaps, shipped across water, through air, your destination as marked, as your interior, one locus of a line of flight of many lines of flight, for which there was no beginning, no end, just those words, worked over through star culled winter lights, the marks and shapes, the patterns on the page the falling bodies of planetary influence, sifted by rapid descent, the magnetic pulse flowing through the ether, the ionosphere, sifting away dimension, gathering as particles of sound made mute where the page holds you, a story of the dead, the killed, the killing, you as you were before, as you were sometime between then and the end, before we killed and memorialized you, before we left you marked, incomplete, shadows on the face of winter fields, still, barely lit, as if from a lamp, behind us, casting forth, waiting for the voice to mouth the words, to enchant the body, with life again, as if to bring you back would matter, as if matter, could be made, re-mattered, to matter again, in the spirit of knowing what was can be again, as if spirit were matter awaiting just a voice, to make what was once matter, matter again.

I hold you in a morning window now. A road beyond, turning into hills, the vehicle gone, you in another window inside, I remain in the house with the old ones, wondering will you come back and if you do, will you remain with us here, where we say so little.

We follow the sounds of deep bells. Bodies move through the church, find pews, sit, stand and kneel. A priest speaks over a body. Who is it this time? Can we call him by the same name? Is he someone else now? Someone else having left for somewhere else? The priest continues speaking filling the body with words, filling the surrounding satin interior, your very clothes, filling the casket he lies in, with words that we will lift and carry to hole in earth, to the cemetery, where we bury all of our words, with more words floating above the dead, the words we buried them with, until there is nothing left to say, as if the ground itself has become the place of words and the world above where we walk around, remains silent, feeling the ground underneath, speaks for us all.

ANOTHER SPIRIT FIRE UNDER EMPIRE

(This is How Your Father Dies)

You meet tradition again
in an airport waiting area
this time

An old Otter Tail Pillager
boarding school and viet
nam photos in some white
clay closeted box

An IRA birthdate
tattoo on
an inside forearm

He's returning to White Clay
a brief layover in Minneapolis
We begin our conversation
over separate coffee tables
near departure gates

Where you from?
Moves to tribes bleeding
into 21st century memories
people in common
We end with
Ceremonies old
witnesses of fires
no longer burning
lodges he will no
longer go into

He's going back to
places he should have never left
me leaving for a place
I should never have gone.

It wasn't ineffective
medicine that killed the old
man, or some belief
gap we fell through
as travelers but fires
of our own making
still burning but with
fewer to hold us together
in story or talk.

Back Before We Returned to White Clay

My Aunt shot my Uncle X

took his insulin syringe
full of bear grease

drove hummingbird needle
deep into the indian hills
left subdivision of his
ass as he slept off tumblers
of liquored remedy
for another frigid
minnesota, just this side
of north dakota, biboon
night

The grease ran into him
filled blood ways with
thicker than what are
the almost insoluble
animal insides, slogged
him down into the deep
dull hull of the craft
and aged curve of his
father body

Brought him
to life in a winter where
we heard the sound
the music of his

language dissipate
his eyes the moon shone
apertures
of our own
lasting longing for
more words

THE ARCHER UNCLE

Forgive him for shooting
the black cloud with
the yellow thunder arrow
He was my Uncle once

And then he chose to
travel to the village
where the only firekeeper
burns the tip of some
braided hair of the earth
feeds flames from
shadows against a
backdrop of northern pines
pointing out the arrival of autumn
sky

As if our animal clothes
and buried human skin
could not cover well enough
our transitions
woman to sky
man to bear
body to light
road to moon
celestial archer
to radiomagnetic
astral belts and pots
The dying fusion and explosive
galactic Dwarfs
tightening and simmering
an ever-expanding universe

of sound, color, the very
calendars of our lives
still and storied in our
looking up

The arrow as you might recall
broke open the day
showed houses we thought
as one kind of home
holding unsettled remainders of dreams

Uncle never gave up
He kept fighting for light
a way out of the darkness
He gave his breath always
to good words
even at the end
of the summer of lost
organs

He gave people
gathering together
ways
to remember home
how We left and how
We can go back
in words around
a Fire

THIS WILL BE YOUR LAST
CEREMONY, YOU THINK

the fire keeper yawns
as he presses cedar against coals
in the base of a shallow pan

you push your face closer
to the smoke
breath in

inside the arbor singers
whisper leaning over
a song is coming
this way

beyond the southern door
children run into twilight
small plastic monsters
army men and tiny vehicles
in their palms

SPIRIT MATTERS: IN REMEMBRANCE

Venus Zhaawanigiizhik sings through
a reserve of bodies
at the mouth of the largesse of rivers
We feel it in our corpses
the untended crops of earth life
the sun passage signs lettering
the faces of passing seasons
the dark room conversations
exposed in morning light as
all the love we have been longing for
in the children we were made
in the children who made us
in the unpronounced blessing
of the good life people as
old as remembrance remains
storied in our dawn land migration
to where we remain in remembrance
not dust to dust
nor this is just to say
not as though the residual matter
of anything
of image matters

We remain in remembrance
Prayer carriers we carry
what we remain in remembrance
away from fires
of the smallest of liberations
We remain in the smallest of
liberations great enemies of
s.c. replicants

replicants of settler colonial
replication

Musing Travelers Musing and the
great enemies of settler colonial replication
the smallest of liberations

Let us become image
as we were before matter
remade us with
objects of distraction
words traveling
on emotion more
than deeper older
sounds of storied
being stored within
us

Shadow Boxes for Zahquod

X was still a laughing boy
Our Aunts crooned country songs
between ice cracking and the yellow
house Relative V burned

When X wept for childhood
Buick died, Asinik went
to Nam and the old empty
Grace Hotel
spewed dust when we
entered

When X seemed an adult disaster
you could smell the anger
in his speech hear the liquor
in his words

Let me tell you
how he died

There was this
white house
he went in

When K was brave boy
he guarded the outhouse
for the girls who didn't
want makoonce sneaking
up on them

When K was fighting for love

he liked to sing
we just disagree
as he split wood
for *Here and There*
Woman

When K was afraid to kill
he brought me to fight
Asinik but Asinik ran
and no one's seen
him since

When K was holier than catholic
we skipped altar boy
practice and went to
the ball field to
watch old brooklyn
cubans hammer higher
arcing shots of
tailing Anishinaabe
fastballs and hanging
curves
in deep drives all the way
to the creek in front of
the episcopal guild hall

Even as I hold this
handful of dirt
standing here next
to these brothers
we have no song
to bring you back

as if you've gone across
the water again
this time with no
leave
to return to us
scattered as we
are

SUDDENLY COUSIN X

surrenders to

a ghost pepper
chicken wing

with micro beer

a franchise inside
a restaurant
inside a casino

your aunt wanders
alone
looking for someone

there
a week ago

you tell her
he's home
watching the Gophers

UNCLE X

makes another
afternoon

another longhouse
reconstruction

from the rematriation
of unearthed artifact images

symbols for wind
fire, heat and cold
a nameless archer
(no target)

time shattered vessels
pieced together

a winnowing basket for
letters

shaken to make words

the lighter consonants lift
taken in updraft

heavy long vowels
open up small sleeves of sound

as though time and space
are calling us by secret
names to older bodies

where dark and light are
at war and heat and cold
won't relinquish to
change

this is how it goes
the image the spirit

the instruments
the sound

sing this way
sing this way
sing this way
sing this way

Venus Zhaawanigiizhik Tries to Kill
(POV Uncle X)

The Moon cast window struck
South Dakota souvenir
ashtray spun mid-air

The cigarette still smoking
fiery red lipstick still clinging
to one fiber filter end, the camel
separating, falling, in smoke
in spark trail glitter of glow,
the orange

coals of a fire bed
a bedroom of
little fireworks, cascading

onto wood floor, a throw of
fake pueblo carpet weaving

the glass disk
Coming toward me,
carrying bloody,
ends, intent words never
could commend
a point of impact at
the same third eye
i dreamily passed through

night after night after day
after day after night day

day night the unmarked
inseparable blend of random
image-making with an
unknown maker

to build scenes
rez edged fields
horizons of hills
dead family on the
other side
to make theatre
curtains of color
a stage of ghost
supper tables
where food and stories
live together at
the edges of every memory
of every relative gone
window on scene
behind the table
leading to a road,
a river, whatever moon
calls to shine upon
against whatever earth
spins to shine upon
or eye i used
to make an imagined
shot from a
bow the arrow
an eye going to
a golden hart
bounding betwixt

and between
oak and maple
ironwood, ash, the
fallen beech, the standing
dead elm
the fright of a deep
startling wound
tearing skeins of breath,
a passioned flight of
how to stay alive
just by keeping oneself moving
past all final exits

Until the end makes
itself my own
the glass ashtray
Strikes a head
then i too am called
away vacuumed into
dark interiors bad
 wall paneling
household kitsch
framed platitudes
verses, white jesus,
on the wall

tribal art, the kind
old relatives give you
the kind you put out
and couldn't get rid of
at a rummage
sale, even if you threw

in a hammer and nails
a crucifix your grandmother
once came at you with

At the last,
seeing the cigarette still
smoking, the moon out the
window, Venus Zhaawanigiizhik
across the room her
face unmasked rage
as if my going and her
staying were the only end
to not listening
especially while she's so
deep into drink and a camel
nothing else matters

INTERLUDE:

An Uncertain Longing

Broken Table of Contents
From Zahquod's
Book of Dreams

The Unlit
Summer Lives
Of Fireflies
White Clay Premonitions
From the Yet to Be Born
Dirt in the Mouths
Of Angry people
Sparrows exit
The Steeple
Vibrating Bells
Last Communion
Songs of Dead Relatives
An Unremembered Colorless Road
The Toy Arrows
The Heart Never Found
The Animals Inside
The Ancient Rabbit Syllabary
What We Said Before
Sleep as an Invention
Of tomorrow as it Never Was

The Song I Wanted to Write is Traveling

seeking the red sun road, to pick up the passenger whose dreams time grinds to salt and tears, to stop wherever the last flash of intuition flares up shadows across landscapes memory won't hold, as if any or all of this were writing, anything, but what we cannot say, is not love, is not hope, is not the light circling, an invisible center, perhaps to find an illuminated singer therein, with a gift to give.

DISTANT OTHERS

LETTER TO COUSIN X

We must not labor skin for promise dream for passage through comfort to some grave beyond.

Tell your lover who left you for dead or, worse, worth less than her desire, you remain alone
most of the time an old singer whose songs turn dance to eyes eying those storms ahead, or break motion part by part to slow the whirl of girl and boy, the staid and regal strut of woman, man, any of them, of us, to more simply expressions on faces on changing surfaces, planes, sky, the land.

As for the old one who told you absolutely, *with no love waiting on the other side, you'll find it's hard to cross over, with no conductor to conduct you, with no impulse to pursue, as love guides you over, as some double arc of you who still loves, the one you think of, thought of, as loving you, there across waiting to make the arc with someone else.*

As for the father who told you once *you are not my son* and from your mother you heard the same: they picked you up once when you were lost, brought you to quiet, saw you into sleep, drove you into the hills and north in winter, spring and summer to hear the old ones, the singers and dancers, the diviners and lonely thunder powered clowns who took you in as well.

You've had as many loves as any man, as many as hurt allows as many who thought they want the best and showed by effort that the one you believed to be your one love was never with you, when loss is everything that remains of your face as you pour liquor into your throat drowning mockery, dousing laughing echoes with just enough burn to keep a fire going inside

AMONG THE ALMOST DECOLONIZED

You remain one of ten
Brothers of weapons lost

In a land devoured by myths
of strangers devoted

to regimes of pulverized
matter fed to abused
animals fed to men

and women who survive
with ether blasts of particles
of a remembered better

all tethered to Stone lions
guarding the entries
to libraries and museums

We must return
to find ourselves
after long stretches

in enslavement

True sunrise
comes over the
the backs of relatives

cloud elders, the first
bringers of light running

morning behind them
hill people, river people,

ridden
with dreams and
vague recollections
of songs for taking
water into copper
bowls and containers
cut from between
the eyes of trees
petitioned for
forgiveness

as with a language spoken
only once a day for
millennia of relations

we now ask
in another language
for the location
of our weapons,
our relatives,
with the very
words keeping
us bound
floating just out of
the reach of
those very places

THE MUTE SCRIBE RECALLS
SOME TALKING CIRCLE

Unsettled by lies and coated with dust, a few lost species have returned
to the fire to speak of lives outside the cast of time and flow of image invested
in our own sense of the visible. Though we stand in mute astonishment their
language reaches us in hints and implications, translated, at times in light
bands, or shifts of cold and warm, often by wind, as when a few smaller
whirling leaves circle, caught in conversations of seasonal turn. This tells us
something bigger approaches, not quite tornadic, a wider swath of cyclonic
energy, we feel this in our heads as an intense pressure pushing outward as if
to let out the false face dancers we've restrained in friezes of denial and the
exotic comforts of technological asylum in squares and plazas, pixels and
projections of hungry looking women and men who have feasted on every
imaginable plate of planetary gift and resource.

The lost bird reminds us of migration, pathways of water seen from the air as
guide, a magnetic compass of some sort, as best as we can understand in their
attempts to explain flight, journey impulse and sign. The dead flower relates,
regeneration, regulation and aspiration connected to helio force of growth
nurtured in earth-spread subterranean darkness, but light seeking, carbon
breathing, air exhaling, drawn from earth, from a earlier astro genesis of
remagnetization in a long ago, forgotten place, renamed now, again within
the limits of what we understand more as mark and sign than as vibration
and heat.

The golden jackal wields another story, like a torch gesturing face to face, as
words flow in some pyronic allegory, to threaten and chase the still beating
heart back into a darkness of fear, some caved encryption of walls signed by
image older than the narrative passages of human talk.

The woman from the glittering place stories draws air rings unleashes a story liberating clouds from gambler cachets. She sings herself away in a few moments of thickening smoke, almost the reverse of how she said all of her people came here.

At the end of the day all this deliberation leads to starlight, fireflies, whispers and shadows, a husband barking at wife, a wife screaming, one of the marrying speakers carrying original instructions, enters a four-door vehicle and leaves, no goodbye, no language to acknowledge a final exit from this wisdom circle. He just took all his instructions, those old ways and left town in a dark buick.

We Regurgitate Diagnoses

an outline of what kills
is killing will kill us

still no one speaks
of what brought us
to poison what turned
us to chemical living

the heartbreak sunrises
of tongues papered
with liars histories
the histrionics of
denial flooding our
communities with
pipeline runoff
mineral sludge

there are
of course their
death sentences
articles of impairment
ill pronouns fixed to
inflamed abstract terms
the afflicted native noun still
human until some
predicate condition
doctors won't speak of
either seals
or signs

assigns the body
to an unconditional
pose ability

even those among us
who have gone on
in becoming
becoming one of them
replicant speakers
regurgitating diagnoses
never acknowledging
what brought us to
this inhuman language
we come too well to understand
as what kills is killing
will continue to kill

I Have Streamed the Arcane Mother Tongue

swallowed the wind with breath of crows
timed the world by struggle with insufferable phantoms

the whole of memory
even the literal forgotten

but human we are
time the subjects
reimagined remembrance
of place, people, a cold
dive into a river
I won't say of dream
I won't say of pain
I won't say of words
like the how of what
we forgot to say
but no the no
of a way back
to what once was
I won't say

the last acts of one
time memory breaking into
new memory not the more
recent but even the older
of memory more recently
recalled

so I must work from the
whole to manage fragments

conversation at the door
of a church
water songs at
periphery of fire
words at the edge
of glance
departure on a night
so long ago

my unowned longing

a person who lived once
just as well in the telling
part of the untold whole

I still try to tell it all.

THE AILING MEDICINE COMEDIAN'S
POSTCOLONIAL DEATH SONG

You who I used to call Tree
forget about your losses
sunlight, seed, blossom, leaf
There's a black coat on a hook
by the front door you can
wear it through winter
there's a pack of lucky strikes
in the left breast pocket
for you

You who we used to call Apple
call the relative you've
fallen so far away from,
the one sleeping
in the little room above,
a dead clock
and a phone
bedside

You who I used to call
Too-Much-Woman
I promise not to call
You anymore
at least not until I've
wandered long enough
to find the address
with your real name

You who I used to call Brings Dirt
into the House
take off your shoes
shutup
and watch the big screen
tv, T'Wolves are playing
A grainbelt and salami
and crackers wait on the coffee
table, empty the ashtray,
Push aside my
alabaster eagle before you put
your feet up, if you would

You who I used call Woosintoon
everyone I know says
the world doesn't belong to you
you don't have enough gods
to put in every space you sell
so, here's the deal
if I talk to your
wandering, wondrous holy
father
I'm going to tell him
your torturing history
of alien origins
and read him your science of
devolving tales of lost tails
just to move him to smite the
crap out of you, or to tie you
to a whining, steel guitar backed,
country western singer
for the rest of your days
of empire avarice

You who I used to call Fire
whichever way smoke goes
I'm heading in the other direction
I don't have time to chase
after those who refuse
to carry prayer for you

You who I used to call car
one road always leads to another
filling station, one filling station
always leads to standing coffee
donut seductions, lotteries

You who I used to call body
old friends wander through the
interior, scheming behind my back
transforming old habits into
new nefarious cells, chiseling
habits of movement,
like laughter at lame jokes about
limp parts, into canals and fissures
of posed problems and puzzlement
over insolubles
rivulets of dry tears, creases of
some long-forgotten crises,
all the unmentionable atrophied
regions of the withering gods
of muscle and the decay
of bone temple architecture
or the scorched dendrites of chemical
love letters and the snapped synapses

of communication corrupted by too
damned much information and not enough
Sun or sublime time.

You who I used to call memory
forget everything I said and did
winter comes plotting
new layers of earth, longer days of
darkness, a gradual sleep
for some supposed season of renewal
and all relatives travel a road of smoke
and music, prayer and lies,
and look homeward as all relatives
all must

You who I will call epigraph
leave it at this

As you turn away
From this we call
Life of this life
Calling to us
Know there remain
Many horizons even
In looking straight up

Large Provocative Answers

Wings and air
Experiment without the hand
Passengers without destination
Once the dream is told you can never
Return to who you were

Wind through curtains
Meditation before theorem creates theorem
Smashed winter glove in the road
One finger pointing south
I was a crow lifting from a dirt road
It was sundown or august
I was never a crow again

Breeze across the face
The formula remains a closed set
The theatre an open hole there
A woman dipping a brush in red paint
Parts of the landscape we never see
Particles of dust

The road behind the smoking tempest
A bad exhaust

Wind against window
So many sets against so many poses
Threads connecting god man woman child
Horse star, bear star, swan star, road star, fisher star,
A hole in the sky
An event a horizon
The first colors of how many colors

Per second per feet per capita perfect

The questions remain
You've seen with a thousand eyes
A thousand suns
What timeless energy
What unseen light
Opened the hot
southern door
To the house of dancing relatives
As if your hand
Had a hand in it?

GIVEN THE CROWS GLIDING ABOVE ME

and the surreptitious curses
surrounding this empire

I must be traveling
again with no Star
to follow to nowhere
rising up dark stairs
between walls of just the
glint of glass of photographs
as still lights burn on the horizon

Old women collapse
into iron
beds still dressed
Old men set awake
grasping in the dark
for a glass in just
enough shine of
moon to make a mirror
of a window over a
table of tired faces
tangled in tree
and the smoke
at the end of its reflective
reach.

I have completed a cycle of
drinking thirst drinking
feasting and fighting
Of an incalculable chemistry
Of I's past

The drunken mirror
The sober interlocutor
The spirit tethered
to a fire-starting prayer
The decaying
weighing the lesser of two
dishonest comforts
the one refusing to
hear the reaching Crow
Woman reaching in a voice
for words passing words
words passing words
trying to lock in on the
one right word passing word
not should, not must, not would
not could, but words passing words
without harm, or possibility of
misinterpretation of intentions,
but still, exactly, words passing words
to refine, sift, measure, cast, the precise
without any possibility for
leaving any doubt about the
difficulty of reaching into, through
this night for a way to make
One realize the Other must
hear a voice exactly this
way and this way only.

Somewhere long ago
I read
    Remember the others
    Remember the other side

In the margins
Of a nervous script
Of this book of stories
Of stolen children, lost lands,
Removal of organs and bodies
And villages and tongues
Between the pages
Someone put a cedar
leaf

So Crow So long
singing ascends
passes through a few
wisps of smoke
turns back toward
the sound of water
I must interpret all
this as this is how
it must be
before I travel again.

Mahtoha's Futile Attempt
to Decolonize
the Western History Meeting

Speaking from a circle within a circle

An indigenous mind inside
A plains cranium
Calling upon a lamp lit
From fires before

Inside a felt cowboy
hat band surrounded
by 21st Century
urban beadwork

He refers to his Chair
In Vermilion the absent
white peers who
would rather not enter
this conversation of
oppression
fear others face
to face a subject of
large narrative distortions

the distilled biases
of managing how and
where and when
and what of
We speak

We know Matoha
We know
We know this
We have been living
in colonies
for so long

even our mothers
and fathers
looked into
their mirrors

and could not
see behind them
in the mirror
in the room
through the dire
winter windowed
beyond

where the colony
began where the
colony ended

SPEAK DEAR DESERT CROW

word spark
of love settler love
colonial replicant love

like some saddened
postcolonial anti-
gone
mourning at brothers
grave edge

must we always
acknowledge
the body
whether other
or our own
as if no other
were ever ours

our own but
in this deep
deep love of settler
colonial body
blown back to
bits and performance
white clay parts
replicant extracts
of our bodies removals

Postcolonial Dream Abstract
(Blue Shadow Uncle Sings the Sun Down)

the inexpressibles
      stand at the perimeter again
      (what you call boundaries remain the formal claims
      of ownership culture)
attacking with jars of searing heat
bone burn light and time hole cannons of biomass decay
(what you really want to express remains
music without topography)

i say keep breathing
without saying how
      (rhythm to vibration)

turning leaves turn to leavings

our family here adheres to celestial flash rituals
even the ghosts mostly come back when sun goes
and their feedings are seasonal appointments
      (what you call memory remains the interfusion
of moment gone with reminder here)

with an overhead map
the father returns when daystar has gone down
even though the mother seems to rise with birdsong
the song itself coincides with

the inexpressibles closing in again
with forced air
and ultraviolent streams of heat and image

they want our stripped-down time
our ideas, our best material, our presence-past spoken of
and future-given spoken for

still, i carry a grandfather song
a grandfather gave to you too once
i sing again as they come for clothes,
for body, for man, woman, child, for all those
in-between

their own inexpressible unattainables
in the song a grandfather gave me once.

Venus Zhaawanigiizhik Once Said

There will be people who
talk with their eyes
buried in beautiful
distraction

A sunset the tail
of a residual animal
becoming rain
cloud over a wing
dark fields patterned
cultivated
sun slats
through a window
frame

Some will remember
Some will want a photo
A reminder of
where
were
who
was
us

The words
the subject
like
lost seeds of
light unopened
in another's eyes
as forgotten

Love Letter
Delivered by Muskrat

You will find
no earth in paw here
nothing to recreate
from mud breath blown
across a turtle shell
surface

nothing to make
from antediluvian dive
into depths
This time welling
from generations of
tears the pearled
pain of past histories
So deep even muskrat

would find no bottom
in such profound
memory of loss
and its unnameable
assembly of myth
thought
and unthought

Take the paper
folded held
in the black digit
pinch of this mythic
swimmer

Hold it to your
summer eyes
englamoured
Breathe first
syllables, sonic
affirmations their
very vibrations coursing
golden vowels
of all the love I have
for you through you
in swimming to you
deeper into the ever
flowing
chambers of your
luminous heart

I Want to See You

The rivers crossing a dreamers way
to the gypsy woman's autumn rebirth
under a signature of iron cloud sky

Maybe we breathe the same hard
sites of departure opening to snow
as black crow mourning road
runs to sky metal steel doors
behind which singers pound
from intertribal to older beats
and language of songs for everlasting life

Maybe we forget then breathing remains
with us as though we are at the bottom
Of a deep spring of life hoping
to resurface alive once more subjects
bright as sky as the names of those before us,
dreamers dreaming us into this life before
we even knew what living was.

Catalonian Square, Palms and Light

I am the parting embrace of the lost animal at the descent into
the La Gracia metro
You remain under promenade shadows, passing the silver bodied
enchantments of mute street performers, some still reptiles, others
plated heads peering over tabletops, still others in the costumes of euro
gods, juggling clouds

I am steering a small boat through the fog opening beyond the bow of
the two-masted ship
in the Spanish harbor
You hold close to the sun kneaded sand tracking your movement
toward stores of Des Igual pastels wrapped around the bodies of
aluminum manikins along La Rambla

I am at the edge of a plaza, waiting
A square of light, of palms, of sangria, beneath an arch, held
breathless, by longing, once again
You turn from the stands of artisans,
the vendors of jewelry, the Oceanside painters, the home fired ceramics
glazed with copper, arrested in a flow of heat, you walk toward me,
past the fountain of sunned coins, cigarette wrappers and children on
their knees peering into water

I would give mineral life to you, if I could but strengthen blood and
bone, with iron and breath and fire from the heart and an open chest
unlocked by the promise of prayer of faith against fortune, if I could
but enliven our last days with deeper longer hours, together, where
memory brings us without misgiving, or an unacknowledged presence

You will live this way in me, day by day, days to come, as days gone,
remain just with us

You and I
animal
shadow
breath
as memory
a place of light
holding us together

THE LAKE UP NORTH

always lines to fill
in darker corners

to move to

then a side of your face
unsheathed sunlight
draining into
the hollow of an eye
circumscribed gray and
green

a pool deep enough
to hold still swimming
children and animals
lost to summer nights

WHAT REMAINS

Of all names I've written
In dust

Your name remains in part
A long vowel separated

Love completely gone above
A streak of I

In moonlight wood
surface beneath circles
of
two glass
bottoms circular
impressions almost touching

DEAR FIREFLY

Will it be you?
Who will kiss me
Hold me love me
In the pop song place
Of no nonsense?

Like I've always
said never try to sing
the unknown extended
cause of crow limb
hopping
out from tree
a wristwatch in one
wrinkled corn colored
claw shining over water
of some distant pond

where you make out an
image of a lone man
paddling water stirring
as if water were soup
memory water
and the paddle
a kinetic longing
for finding and fishing
the deeper unknown
beneath held ghosts
only a filament,
a line a prayer an
offering could bring forth
before the image and water

together make shore
beneath the crow gone
clouds

Were that man image me
would you meet him at the
shore for sure
to hold me kiss me
love me in the cedar
smell of wind rubbing
sounding like sick
violin trees?
Until
all nonsense gives way
to the heat and hotter
love of your ever burning
star light flickering as if far off
in the distance but held so
close, you, me the heat,
remain in a seemingly
eternal no nonsense
embrace

MEMORY SONG FOR A
WOMAN AT THE SOUTHERN
DOOR

as though flame held
name
in mind for space
in dream contained

I carry you through
mist, rain, the cover,
the openings
and orders of days
held by what carries
us neither
in clothes or skin

as if housing for
memory were
door
shut-in or walled
or windowed out
to wandering
field or autumn
orchard

to the hill
beyond horizon
as some subject
held in finite
number

of breath of days
or sun

i know more of you
than all this given
to time
or time to
tell

RAIN I ALMOST REMEMBER

The last time
I slept in the

before
And the after
Thunder rattled

A dark mirror
Trembling
A wall

Everything hanging
There as if
There to fall

ONLY LYRIC REMAINS CAPABLE

Morning wind smoke

Of not objectifying
You remain
Other through Self
before the glass
through other self
behind the rattling window
though lyric supplanting
self, absent, other
a reflection of oak, crooks of poplars,
the shiver and shake of bird gone
                              branches
with natural phenomena
still looking
as sensing self
as if coming
as another intuiting
rain
self from natural
phenomena
had already reached you

alone in an interior

darkened by sky

                    an approach of clouds

                    too heavy for air

                    to hold.

SOVEREIGNLY EROTICA

A 2nd generation sofa
A blanket of moon
and wolves thrown over
the back

A dining room table
marked by cups
sunlit scratchings
An abalone ashtray
A fuming cigarette
curling blue
follow me smoke
fingers into a hallway
where we hung image
relatives to remind us
where dreams lie

The floor strewn with
fallen treaty pages
agreements lost in less
than acts of love
before bookshelves
with histories of candles
baskets, fetishes, blue
thunder boys fed by
early sunlight passing
glances and searches
for words that may have
moved you through love
and schools for piling
the dead into rooms

and labels like loss
hope, flickering still in
some living embrace
with some barely separable
someone who will
continue to speak to
you from large in
between distances

I won't tell you if
this is not love
the language of
the body just giving
way to entanglement
to some who body
who might take
hold of us and
remain with us
in some everlasting
remainder of shapelessness

of night coming on
offering to give us
away to open doors
roads away to
moonlight with just
a stilled shine of us
releasing unburied
howling
a breath of sound
holding us together

Uncle X Like Virgil Needs His Own Guide

when shapes get shadowy legions
of peculiars
come out to dance to initiate the
growth of melons, buds and blossoms
to shake stones and gourds, to hide
in hides and plumage, the mirage
and hot lick of fire shimmers
to twist and thrust, extend and
hyperextend, limb and lip, shaping
exhalations with open O's of
mouth, open U's of uh huh
to appropro create
in masks, making more in mask to mask
moon rapt howling in dog dark
bark passes
to make animal time in the place of human
nothing

i've marked territory
re-marked
text
lied to love
loved to lie

Venus Zhaawanigiizhik remembers
my better days
from embittered waste
to the lust tangles
to the techno ohm
hum of human some-
things machines

someone inside machines
going as far as sound
can take someone
to silence, or some place
of human nothing

she gave me papers
smoke, mirrors, clubs and pistols
I had the maps but
didn't follow them
didn't look at the legends
paid no attention
to those elevation numbers
passed over symbols for rails
and campsites

I went out on my own
started talking
started answering back
the shadows
started going off then
one by one
knowing at any time
I might join them
as they all made way
to the river
it's moonlight tongue
shining like the eyes of
Venus Zhaawanigiizhik

just trying to get myself
across to some

stranger but better
other side
where becoming animal
remains us becoming
all human

PASSING THOUGHTS OVER A FIRE
(DEAR CROW WOMAN)

As if from dead
and distant fading names
You must forget
strawberries,
if you happen
to hear the meadowlark
calling you toward sunned streams

you must forget the yards of
growing grandchildren
summers hollering sundown

as you must forget
the moonlight, brushing
your hair on the iron
bed while the old man
listened to the narration
of the Twins playing
through the static
and glowing dials
of the radio

Don't try to go back
to grandmother's land,
or back into the house
to turn out bread and
stew for strangers
at the table again.

The water basin remains half-buried
rusting next to the old stove mouthing
weeds and yellow flowers

The memory of your
shaking hands
will be enough
to light a cigarette
for me

I was never a stranger

though
I often showed up
after years overseas,
years and travels
beyond the last address
you saw under my name

Uncle X is still fighting
in one country
For another nation
none of us
belong to
Virgil has crossed over
by canoe, bridge,
or beam of light, crying
or smiling
Who can say?

Zahquod remains on
the other side too

Still summoned sometimes
through songs
Like Rounds of syllables
passed on by a shadow
who woke me
from a mourning dream

The body of life holds

a book of dreams
without organs, without
temperature

A book of dreams contains,

few words,
no maps, no territory,
no instruments,
of navigation, or
tools of construction

just old ones
passing
thoughts over a fire

Some will tell you
you
you
you

are moving toward
death, do not stop,

no matter what the season,
do not cry no matter
how lonesome,

though lonesome
makes for living
as much as any condition
of the heart

as long as silence remains
the open whole

for bringing us back
to the singing,
the telling, the loving,
even the violence
of memory can't
subdue

Pick up this note
I left you then
forget the words
remember the shapes
the forms the hand
across the page

the face
lit by a lamp the
old man carried
long ago

lit though fired by

different fuel,
an arcane fuel
in these times
of so many
ways of igniting
color and object

in what might otherwise remain
barely seen, in the starlit
or luminous phases of moon.

That face,
the one I am wearing now
is not the face
of the one who wrote
the note under lamplight.
It is a face
moving toward you
ranging the earth, filling
up with medicine

talking back to fear
touching here and there
a tree a child's hand another
woman stone taking in food

at times imagining
you at a table,
coffee between us
sunlight spreading over
surfaces, bringing bodies
to light you me,

as if in sharing imagining this,

I am making
food words for you,
to go through
this forgetting
You making food
light for me

(DEAR CROW WOMAN)

You could
have told me

How I was
near dead
horses sun beaten
earth shadows
on the horizon

You could
have said

I looked different without
sun in a room where
we hung our heads

You could have
told me

I could not return to
once again the never told
beginning of how we speak
when even we aren't listening

You could
have reminded
me of the ghost licked
bodies inhabiting my
sleepwalker passing
from bed to fixtures
murmuring in walls

behind crooked mirrors

The last wall marked by
stain running into
window deep into
some august hour
so late the gap unto
my next
awakening closes as if
there were never eyes for seeing
above the branched blow
of arms of barren
hardwood over road

What lies beyond starlight
spaces of night so long
such as this

You could have
told me

CLUES TO MY OWN SILENCE

Gesture into days
sunned against
the turnings of crow
shadow hills

An evening
lamp over the head
of a child
holding
a book we read
before we found
the dreaming colors
of our relatives
smiling in the
light opening our
eyes

How we come back
from the road to
our first home
A sadness lingering
as if sound itself
were buried in
the lost to love

Book of Samuel—Chapter Zahquod, Page Unknown

In my last hours my son tried to teach me how to breathe again, to fill a heart with bright light, to allow the light to expand, or contract, the expansion creating greater light, enough to feed a small forest, where memory could move freely, living among shadows, the windswept call of black birds, the electric movement of small animals, between light and dark, the contraction, to make a small hole in the dead middle of the heart, through which all light made from every breath could pass and become the vehicle in which we travel, finding passengers of every kind of loss, remembrance and quiet unexpressed emotion, traveling with us, in one blinding star, just bright enough to light small worlds, where smaller humans, make fires for those just dead.

ZAHQUOD—MY LAST LETTER

the route through this dream feels the inside of the eye
vitreous breaks and makes mirrors smoky
once the occlusion occurs the hidden result makes reading
impossible
the oral one way out of everything flat and marked
as a child born in a mild warm wind

the route through this dream feels like a febrile vibration
rattling inner ear where no sound stays coherent
once word is absorbed and wrung out of air the song, word,
the performance articulate dissipates out of the invisible
into the inaudible, like seeing missed hearing or hearing mist
as a child born into temperature and time

in my last letter to you
there were four codes
one alphabetic
two surface
three a recombinant script
four paths or routes
I wrote forward to stillness
f to d to t to o to s to third s
spaces opened between recombinant forms of course
between lines against thin planes
set upon harder planes, surfaces
holding empty glasses, emergency candles
eyeglasses, a naïve clay vessel layered
with ash, cigarette, with dust from who knows where

the route through this dream feels like skin
the lost layers of growth, undergrowth and overgrowth

once the skin peels away even bone becomes useless in
passages filled with another kind of harder blood—
fixed without flow lasting longer than movement itself
as a child born walking a route to a horizon.

Grandfather says memory loves sense more than sign
pine smoke more than "no hunting"
or a black x in a yellow roadside
circle, river water cold on the tongue more than "rest area."

Grandmother just goes on boiling water, her dress floral
print, a woman moving back and forth between stove and table

until Grandfather quit talking and took food into the same mouth:
he spoke, speculating on memory;
the mouth must be conduit for sign i said
to myself, just as we eat
the sign not "no hunting" or "rest area"
but some sign of closure

Grandmother says eat eat eat
you have a long day ahead of you
and you do you do you do as
the route through this dream goes on and on
words, signs, everything moving against you
as a child born long ago without memory
or words to tell of all you had seen.

I repeat, this route though dream seems like lost memory
a lost eye, sounds, lost words, lost signs, the moon
magnetic, for all the inorganic transcendence of decay
as if covered by skin lit from inside

in my last letter to you
I reminded you of the house we built
of the autumn fire for the feast of those who've
gone beyond sound, sense, sign
I thought of you then and let you know
you should come to the next fire.

still, I have received no answer.

CRUSHED AKIIWENZII
(A DISINTEGRATING GRANDFATHER HOLOGRAM)

Of grief drained ashen
winter face in glass glare of
risen white clay moon

Relatives moving around
inside the other side of the
glass gesture-shadows feeding
on light and air

This once again is the time
to remain with the unspoken
as if all make and matter
dispersed what we never
thought we could never
say our own gestures lost
memory (untended fires) of
what we were as witness
(the unfed thunder child) to witness
(the youth gone in uniform) hope
(the Pembina hymn singer widow)
without belief (the dead in relatives'
talk at the Star Road vigil)

belief an arm
coming to light from shadow
to touch the violet
animal heart
still steaming on the dark
table where those we

shared time and talk with take
all other offerings served up
to remind you
you too are but
passing through

every remaining speck of
ground down sound and light and
color irretrievable
particulates of living body
mind spirit matter
settling
softly on the ever giving
earth with a song and a
name muted by wind
calling the body home.

LETTER TO ZAHQUOD, SPIRIT MATTERS

For all the world of hope
of love and passionate beauty
there remains death and time
signals to sleep in the idleness
of dulled sense, the atrophied convex
of awareness burning down to a single
smaller view

Perhaps of a hillside you passed once
counting flowering clusters of yarrow heads
the spread of mugwort, other plants
Old Crow Woman did not name or turn
unremembered in your ascent
to a billowed cloud back disappearance
on the other side one lone black bird
wheeling, wailing there above.

Perhaps of a profound darkening interior
the lesser shadows of largesse
the acquisitions of years set posed
in a cedar scented dry winter room
in statutes and trophies, timepieces,
readings, paintings and photographs
of you alone of you and everyone else
who seemed to have mattered

Perhaps to just a bare papered wall,
sun striking there, lettering
indecipherable marks of a language

made only for viewing on that wall
as written by that sun,
later, as perception of letters recede,
making faces of simply shadows,
reeling across a surface as you
follow, waiting to find the next face,
figure, formed from some closing grasp
of imagining this as what you are
as what you experience,
as if you were that happening to you,
in that moment when everything fuses,
passing, passed, becoming, yet to be,
the still unknown you, once there,
there, not there, almost there, to be there,
never to get there.

I must tell you I have been
lost to more love in me.
I gave it away or secretly
stored it over the years,
parsed it out among children
who mostly at the time would rather
run in sunlight, delivered it to addresses
of women, relatives and associates
who ignored its worst desiring, designs
and lived off of its better parts
in better times, stuffed it in tree hollows,
under stones, where it remains
hidden to this day, a terma for an affiliate
hermetic, walking ghost robed, through an
immanent future seeking some holy,
as yet undisclosed way to say to someone

who will accept the love you left behind
as a formal invitation to take everything
one can offer in mind, body and spirit
without demanding that you succumb,
succor, suppress or starve to keep it secure,
under the influence of fear and loss.

I must tell you this and more,
more I must tell, for the must must
reinforce love and the more must
more than that release us
from the dire dark and dirty
dreams that haunt us all in all
the hollow empty cores we have
in common in the common we call
family all connected to Zahquod
who left us in suffering
in his and in our own

I wrote this after a long trip west,
to see the going gone off and the still
going, going on in ways the gone
could not have imagined
before or after she left.

Her
name
was
R
or Andegikwe.

Hers and your
father fell
so the story goes
from the sky
and died
on an asphalt
road
a rock hard human
broken in
an instant, with
nothing to grasp
in the fall
he reached
up
found nothing
there.

There are liars among us. That's a given. There remain thieves among us
that's to be taken. And living bodies remain, writhing in nets, dragging iron
traps, from concrete enclosures, through streets of glass and steel, traffic
loops, train platforms, bus fumes, living bodies remain.
we learn from some, take stories from some, hide ours from some. They
remain relatives. This has no beginning or end, in what was said, or what
was taken, what of each body remains, in hiding, unsaid.

Yours and her
father fell from the sky
So, the story goes
and she and I
never knew him.

LET US BE PAINTING, PAINTER, SINGING, SINGING, SINGER
FOR H.E. EPHEMERA

So, "this is poetry," is not poetry. We would rather be verb than noun or object even if the poem brings us to a final word as if settled on image or object image. A flat stone soaking water, a rainfall of women's voices, secret children of muses syncopating, in the weight of clouds running down roads in the passes of August memory. The noun lives in colonies, the verb escapes with a slice of bread taken from a table set, with fruit and a pistol, a shining watermelon glass of Kool-Aid, painting painting painter. Just as we would rather be singing singing singer, the echo coming from some filmy shore as we pass, paddling paddling paddler, gliding without enough names for water, over the surfaces named water, even as we believe this is poetry, even if we believe the event remains too limited, the extended, possibility of no context, no place, just the voice, in a small room, walls of books, rotting clothes, empty subjects, hanging jackets of winter, the voice alone, at a station, perhaps, singing, singer, without enough names for lyric, for an uncertain longing, with sounds we call lyrical, even as the words end somewhere, in the extending impossibility of fixed context, stopping, coming to rest where the noun lives in colonies and the poetry, singing singing singer, coming to rest, now and again, the verb singing breathing breather, breath, without even names for poetry, poem poet, coming to rest, as if we could be poet or anything other than breathing, breathing, breathing, breather, poet, breathing, breath, breathing, breather, poet, breathing, singing, sounding, singing, singer, sounding, poet, singing, the sound, sounding, song, poet, breathing, sound, breathing, song, breather, breath.

TRY NOT TO SAY ESSENCE

As the last name before darkness falls comes from the river way. You remind me of someone who spoke over the table before we gathered for a meal. I have been wearing a face of lost people of the generation who made sharing a code among us who are left with their names, a few blankets from childhood, coins, a ball full of a lifetime of games, a language spoken now by inhabitants of pictures, given to us, in some past, of some distant reserve, set aside for us, always, even as we go on, inside the forgetting and forgotten.

VENUS ZHAAWANIGIIZHIK: SOLILOQUY

(At end of a diminishing
American Spirit Menthol)

It's cascading starlit rain
Lamps and alleys at the
Dead end of urban myth
The lost bodies
Of Little people
The unknown appearances
Of elves
In jinn smoked twilight
Where the vibratory
Casts of poets
And travelling storytellers
No longer make spirit
Matter the way matter
Seems to be
The only finality
Of be
In these days
Of once unimaginable
Unimagined living
And Dead
I call forth
And will not stop
Calling forth

AT TIMES THE DISTANT OTHER

arrives from distance traveled from some distant other

You open the moonlit suitcase and draw distant clothes from distant closets

A beating heart flies bearing west with wings once worn by a distant other

You tell time by the hands separating numbers, lines, hours and seconds
of a distant other

One hand to another distant other hand-held device carrying the voice
of the other

If there were no Gods, no spirit, there would be no life without the distant
other

Yet those so settled in so close make nothings shame

Make no and yes and unbind what names

of each to every of every to many

unknown to one unknowing

near enough to hear the words of the distant other.

Yet to Be Unnamed Arrival

Just before dawn, upon waking
we follow the old people to the water's edge.
We remain there in silence the water-surface a black mirror
the slow drag of stars across its face
Until the first bringers of light appear far off
beyond what anyone could call horizon
The oldest among us, Everlasting Sky sings to bring them in
Awaaso joins in on the second verse, a trembling echo
vibrating as the water surface folds reflections,
under changing colors of the sky

In time, a distant blue speck floats out of the crown of sun
As it draws nearer we know it is one of us, returned in a song,
a canoe we sent out long ago
when we, two of us unknown to history or time by name
embraced, through arms and flesh
the way we should always embrace
with only the thought
of gratitude for the moment at hand,
in the uncoiled arcs of electricity between us
the warmth of fire flashing beyond us, heating our skin with love
for living, for this life we share.

As the canoe draws closer we see the child, wrapped in red cloth
at the bottom of the canoe, eyes open, charging depth and distance
in rush of sky with a deep longing a lasting patience of one who knows
more
of the unknown what it is to arrive here, among the already known,
the knowing and the to be known.

As the canoe touches shore, old woman Besho, slides her hands beneath

The red cloth and lifts the child from the canoe. There is a voice then cry or call,
Singers start up again, father and mother, reach out for the child then,
Holding her beneath the arms, they pull her feet from beneath the cloth
And touch them to the white clay at the water's edge.

By the time the sun has made its way south the child is home and
the people wait, once again
as the old ones submit petitions for a name.

EPILOGUE: CHIAABOOS AT THE RIVER AGAIN

The last of us
remain

standing
at water's edge
waiting for passengers

to fill our silver canoe
to set out toward

the going
down sun
coursing too
sailing
to the other side

through a
A starlit river gone
shine given way
to the nearer brighter
luminary breaking
night over names
traveling over hills
crested by shadows
of Our still sleeping
selves walking into
bodies of light

Remind those on the other side

How the I fed fire,
planted three sisters with
grandparent songs
brought plates of food
into freezing dark for
nameless guests
drew shadow extensions
on a silver veined mountain face
warmed winter children
watered the lips of
a dying mother's thirst

How I caught and swallowed whirls
of dissipating smoke
blew my heart out through
blanched bones in
dessicated
poplar and willow arbors
Slept beautifully in
beds of summer washes

How I split the shadow between
a man and a woman
holding on in the dark space
of a steamy bedroom
of a city driven toward dawn

yet to be made light
yet already lost to what led

to us in the last photograph
of memory
coming out of a closet
a darkroom like a gravedigger's
shovel opening ground
to stories held
beneath every living
surface

ACKNOWLEDGMENTS

"Through the Refuge," *Iperstoria*, Verona, Italy, 2017

"Almost Decolonized," *Iperstoria*, Verona, Italy, 2017

"Dead GPS," *Iperstoria*, Verona, Italy, 2017

"Departure a White Clay Soldier," *Iperstoria*, Verona, Italy, 2017

"Back Before We Returned to White Clay," *Iperstoria*, Verona, Italy, 2017

"The Return of White Clay Brothers," *Iperstoria*, Verona, Italy, 2017

"Let Us Be Painting, Painter, Singing, Singing, Singer For H.E. Ephemera,"
Poetry Magazine, June 2018 and *Native Voices*, 2019

"The Mute Scribe Recalls Some Talking Circle,"
New Poets of Native Nations, 2018

"Dear Uncle X" (Published as "Dear Sonny"),
New Poets of Native Nations, 2018

"A White Clay Relatives Tabernacle of Grief,"
Forthcoming in *Indigenous: A Great Lakes Anthology*

"Dear Crow Woman (You could have told me),"
Forthcoming in *Indigenous: A Great Lakes Anthology*

"Crow You Dreamt Dark from the Name of Fire,"
Forthcoming in *Indigenous: A Great Lakes Anthology*

"It Was Snowing on the Monuments," Poem of the Day, Featured Poem,
Poetry.Org, November 2020

ABOUT THE AUTHOR

GORDON HENRY is an enrolled member/citizen of the White Earth Anishinaabe Nation in Minnesota. He is also a Professor in the English Department at Michigan State University, where he teaches American Indian Literature and Creative Writing. He serves as Senior Editor of the American Indian Studies Series at Michigan State University Press. In 1995 Henry received an American Book Award for his novel the *Light People* and his poetry, fiction and essays have been published extensively, in the U.S. and Europe. In 2004, he co-published an educational reader on Ojibwe people with George Cornell. In 2007, Henry published a mixed-genre collection, titled *The Failure of Certain Charms* with Salt Publishing. More recently Henry's writing has appeared in, *Bob Seger's House*, by Wayne State University Press; *Iperstoria*, a literature journal, from the University of Verona, Italy; *Revolucion: A Cuban Journal*, of Havana; *New Poets of Native Nations*; the June 2018 issue of *Poetry*; *Wassafiri;* and *When the Light of the World was Subdued, Our Songs Came Through* (2020) and *Living Nations, Living Words* (2021)—two poetry anthologies edited by Joy Harjo. Gordon now lives in Empire, Michigan.